"THE QUESTION"

Edwin Gautier Vega

iUniverse, Inc.
Bloomington

"THE QUESTION"

iUniverse books may be ordered through booksellers or by contacting:

iUniverse
1663 Liberty Drive
Bloomington, IN 47403
www.iuniverse.com
1-800-Authors (1-800-288-4677)

ISBN: 978-1-4502-8480-6 (pbk)
ISBN: 978-1-4502-8481-3 (ebk)

Printed in the United States of America

iUniverse rev. date: 1/27/11

"THE QUESTION"

THE QUESTION

One day,

There was a man standing

At the edge of a cliff.

Pondering, he looked down,

And he saw the Lord, JESUS,

Standing below.

Convinced that he needed to find out,

If the Lord loved him and how much,

He looked at the Lord and he proceeded,

To state and then ask, "Lord, I grew up,

Believing and following your ways,

But I need to know and I need to find out,

 If I jump from this cliff,

Will you be there for me?

Will you be there to catch me?"

The Lord,

Not surprised at the man's request,

Immediately extended his arms in front of him

And then the Lord proceeded to state,

"Son, if you need and want to find out,

Go ahead and jump,

That is the only way

That you will know and find out

If I will be there for you!"

The man,

Puzzled and amazed at the Lord's answer,

Gave the Lord a final look.

He turned around and proceeded

To walk away from the cliff.

The man,

Attempted to find truth in his question(s),

But in looking for that truth

While searching for answers from the Lord,

He did what he did,

Throughout his whole life.

He would attempt to find the Lord

And follow the Lord's ways.

He would find him,

But not have enough courage,

Faith and belief,

He turned his back and without trying

Confused, he walked away.

Not realizing

That if he would never had asked the question,

"Will you be there for me?

Will you catch me?"

He would never have needed an answer.

The man did what he should never have done.

In his thought

He searched for wisdom from the Lord, JESUS.

He sought and found the truth.

He however questioned the Lord's wisdom,

But he did so without faith.

THROUGH THE EYES OF A CHILD

Through the eyes of a child

You can see beyond the stars.

You can reach the sky above

You can love just everyone.

Show me how, to lead some day.

Show me how, to reach somewhere.

Help me grow, one year one day.

Will you see, and walk with me.

Hold my hand, don't let me fall,

While I try today to walk.

The road is long, the road is hard.

When you see, what you can be.

The years have passed, I've traveled far.

I've seen the world, I've seen beyond.

Now in turn, I'll hold that tiny one.

Who will conquer all, who will be someone.

I have lived; I now have to die,

But, before, I'll bless the one

Who will be, and who will see;

Through the eyes of a child.

THE ACHIEVER

The mind, like the universe, is a totality in itself.

Both are unexplored horizons that hold secrets
That the naked eye of mankind will never see.

Intelligence and the thirst for knowledge
Expand the human mind beyond reasonable barriers.
Just like the universe, extends beyond its already discovered galaxies,
Beyond barriers that exist in the realms of reality
Far from ever being observed, found and /or discovered,

Mysteries will always exist
In the mind and of the mind.
Mysteries also exist in the universe.

The difference between both, is that one, the universe, is infinitely
 Large and beyond physical exploration and explanation.
The mind being the other,
Is still un-explore-able-ly impossible,
Small with limits beyond explanation,
With an infinity of knowledge that achieves set goals,
Set by the holder of the mind, body and soul of the achiever.

THE DREAM HAS DIED

Tonight, I've thought of you, Martin Luther King Jr.

And I've had to shed some tears,

Because what became reality, perished with you,

killed by an assassins bullet.

You were meant to be the dream.

The dream of all men to be created equal,

The dream of all men to be free.

Free of racism and free of segregation.

Free of hate and free of injustice.

Free of being called a Negro and all the shallow things

That were never meant to be.

You are the dream that wants to constantly continue

To strive and achieve in the People's hearts and minds.

But you continue to die Mr. King every day,

Cause some of your own People

Have become ignorant against each other.

They've become murderers, rapists,

Drug dealers, racists and oppression-ist.

They've simply become what you once fought against.

They've become the nightmare of reality.

They've become the nightmare of your beautiful dreams,

To be free.

Let freedom ring,

But freedom cannot ring and will not ring,

Without your words which will echo,

Day by day, year by year,

Seeking to find listener's who will hear,

Speak, understand and subsequently follow each principal

Of your beliefs, and to eventually embrace your memory,

Martin, so that one can follow your path of light.

Then your powerful un-forgetful voice,

Will once again rise to lead our People towards the promised land.

In order to remind the human race,

Of the old Negroid spiritual of our ancestors,

That continues to march on.

We will the rise in harmony,

Together united, with strength-full, hopeful

And courageous voices.

We will all dare emerge, chanting; "FREE AT LAST, FREE AT LAST,

THANK GOD ALMIGHTY, THAT WE'RE FREE AT LAST."

Believe it Martin Luther King Jr.,

The dream has died, but your words will always echo

While marching from your grave,

Until we are indeed FREE.

TO BE FREE

To be free,

Is to be loved,

With moments of happiness'

achieved.

That is the dream,

That is the feeling of each being.

It is the desire to anxiously get and keep liberty,

Not falsehood while stretching ones existence

To break any barrier,

In order to find love.

That is to be free.

That is to be loved and wanted.

It is liberty and ones existence

That break those barriers in order to reach

And arrive at a state of reality

In the life of a free being.

To be free.

ABOLISH APARTHEID

People from around the world,

Come unite to stop apartheid.

Let us give a helping hand from the Virgin Islands,

To our imprisoned brothers and sisters.

Let us help fight,

The battles of the mind

The wars of the body and soul

In order to have our African People,

Find freedom, Truth and liberty.

Only freeing the land and People

From where once our ancestors departed,

Will we in due time break their slavery chains.

Then all People of the Virgin Islands

And also of the world,

Will break free from the imaginary chains

That tie our hands within our minds.

Let us all unite, to abolish mental slavery.

Let us all united

Also abolish Apartheid

MY BADGE

As a law enforcement officer.

My thoughts are only prayers

That rest upon my shield of pride

For which I've sworn with faith and honor

To protect all need-ies' lives.

I've sworn to use my badge of honor

To bring peace truth and justice.

With honest words that are an oath

And integrity to help it.

With my badge,

I've looked up to GOD

And I've also made a promise.

I've promised to those

That I'll protect,

To gave my life for them.

HIMSELF

One night,

While having a sleepless night,

Due too many problems,

A man had a vision that made a miracle of prayer occur.

The man found himself,

No longer in his room in his bed.

He found himself,

Searching for answers to his many questions.

He found himself,

On a lonely but peaceful beach.

Kneeling while staring at the sky,

Looking at the stars.

He felt a lonely being

And he also saw formed by many stars

The praying hands of JESUS,

Besides the glorious light of the moon.

He then realized that he was in the presence of GOD.

The man then asked the LORD to bless him,

Like GOD had done so many times until that moment in his life.

To lead his every move,

To breathe the man's every breath,

In his,

GOD'S name.

The man then found what he was searching for.

He recalled that from since he was a child,

He had followed the LORD's way by talking to the LORD,

Through prayer.

He also found himself,

Back in bed,

Back in his room without any problems.

He had discovered that through his prayers,

He had answered all of his questions,

Because through the LORD's miracle,

The prayer.

He the man,

Now asleep,

Had found himself.

THE LORD

The Lord appeared to me one day,

While, I sat in thought and prayer.

He then let me know he loved me.

He let me know, he'd always cared.

"I've always been with you my child",

The Lord said.

"From before you thought of being born.

Since, I've held your hand and I've guided you.

I've have seen you,

when you've fall."

"I've helped you up so many times,

I've seen you cry,

I've seen you grow.

I've seen many tears roll down you face.

You've been so brave, to break your falls."

"In my presence my child,

You've brushed all the bad things away,

And you've looked at me and told me,

Lord, you can let me fall today,

You've built love,

hope and strength in me."

13

The Lord with a smile then continued,

"My child,

I know that you really trust me,

And I know you've strength to fall,

And strength to keep on going,

But since I've been there to help you,

And I've guided you for so long,

I see no reason at this juncture,

My child,

To let you fall without me.

For I need your hands in prayer,

Which I refuse to let go of,

Because,

I will always be there to love you,

Like you my child has been there to love and cherish me,

And trust me with your most powerful and beautiful prayers,

I Love you my child".

The Unknown Author

THE CONSCIOUSNESS

The consciousness of a society is failed,

When a dictatorship takes its place.

Then suffering minus justice equals and becomes slavery and possible death,

By orders denied and correct laws unapplied,

Causing the slavery chains to return to seek the free and just.

For the "ORDER" denies others,

For the power is that of the enemy

And the wrongful owners of the mass of wealth,

Have pity for none outside its ranks.

Every step taken forward, will be reversed by 11 backward,

For the eyes of evil will dare reverse,

The good will of mankind,

And the cries of the majority will be heard.

For it is because of the Majority that sided with the "ORDER",

For the Majority sought to comfort its master(s),

Not knowing that they sought to harden their spirits and souls,

By selling their vicious souls and persecuting those that seek the truth,

The ones that fight for the consciousness of it's' society, and its perishing survival.

DRESSED IN BLUE

He was put on earth by GOD

Blessed with an oath, a badge and pride

With faith and dressed in his office blues,

While thoughts of law, passed through his mind.

A mission from GOD is his given job

To protect life and property

While bring truth , peace and justice

To the eyes of GOD and man.

He walks the streets with pride.

Giving and showing respect,

Helping the aged, loving the kids

Not showing his loneliness.

To some he's called a cop.

To others a beast or a pig.

To many he's just a beautiful person,

Who honors with integrity, the minds of both GOD and men.

I'm one of those who has dressed in blue

And I know down deep inside

That GOD always has me in his hands

And some men in their prayers.

NOW, THINK ABOUT THAT!

It is not by chance nor by accident

That we meet people,

But, by destiny.

For we meet people,

To somehow help

Learn and assist each other

And to be one another's healers

Advisors, counselors and among other things

Each others' Guardian Angels.

We meet in good times

And bad times

To learn from each other.

Whether it be in a positive or negative

Way or light

When one has taken the wrong turn

Arrived at a new place

Gotten into an accident

Or just simply

Been; in the wrong place at the wrong time.

Like I said, "By destiny".

For we are chosen

To be each other's guardian angels

To show each other

What should be the proper direction?

Or somehow find the end of our destination.

As free willed individuals,

There are several questions that we need to ask ourselves;

"Are we indeed listening to our guardian angels of destiny"?

"Are we taking their advice and following the proper path,

That is being shown,

For our own good and benefit"?

Or are we meeting the negative People,

Death, destruction and total demise?

WILL THERE BE JUSTICE?

Freedom,

The desire of all men

Granted to some of its people

By the new world.

With the ability to be free,

The law of man sought impartiality and equitability,

With the scale that has been unbalanced for decades

And held by a blindfold lady

Called, "Lady Justice".

Wealth, race, religion, color and creed,

At times determined the final chapter of injustice,

However, the law of GOD, supersede those laws,

Creating a path of light, abandoned by men,

Society and the lady.

This world with time

Will undo itself

And her honor will perish.

Our land will someday return to basics

To Principles'.

Our homeland and its' people

Will again be free.

Because the final authority, GOD,

Will indeed assure most,

That the scale be balanced.

He will speak and practice

Impartibility and equitability.

Then the oppressed,

Will find real liberties

Within our laws,

And men will forget

About greed and power.

Then and only then,

"Will there be Justice."

WHILE THINKING ON WHAT TO SAY

While feeling the warmth of your body besides,

While looking at the dark blue sky,

And hearing the roaring waves,

While,

I'm thinking on what to say.

My thoughts go far beyond that sky,

While admiring some sparkling stars,

I love at first,

Then love goes like waves,

While,

I'm thinking on what to say.

I want to gave you all I've got,

And go beyond the sky for love.

The waves go back to the sandy shore.

While,

I'm sharing my life with you,

And while I'm thinking,

On what to say.

TO BE, A MOTHER, TO BE
(MY MOTHER)

One day,

In the past,

Present or future,

You, my mother to be,

Made love to a man,

That would possibly be my father.

There were many caresses

And many silent moments,

There in the heat of passion

Experiencing pleasure,

You were now on your way

To be,

A mother to be.

Several weeks

And days went by.

By now,

You knew you had conceived.

You knew that I was on my way,

But he my father to be

Was no longer there by you,

You, my mother to be.

More days and weeks went by.

By now,

You'd started to cry.

For you loved him like no other.

But he showed,

He'd never care.

"I'm going to have a child",

My mother thought.

"A child without a father."

She was hurt

And thought of an abortion

For days,

She wanted to kill the pain

That was there within,

She wanted to get revenge.

I felt a great rejection,

That was separating me

From my mother to be.

My mother was thinking of killing me,

Me!

Her child to be.

I started to move

And to cry in silence.

I started to shout,

But my shouts all went unheard.

I felt anger towards my mother.

I started to mentally fight and struggle,

Against her thoughts,

Against her will.

Because, I feared for my life.

Because nature was making me understand,

That you only have

An opportunity

To live

Just once in life.

Somehow,

I let my mother know

That life is very precious.

I concurred her love,

Her love from within her body.

I did so in desperation.

"MOM,

Don't be a killer, MOM.

Please don't think of an abortion.

Forget the first mistake,

That you made with him.

Don't make the second one with me."

"Please MOM,

I want to see the world

And feel, breathe, taste and hear,

And embrace you in my arms,

One day,

The (that) day that I am born".

Today is the day of my birth,

And I've seen your joyous expression.

"Mother, you've given me the gift of life

And for that I have to thank you.

I will ask the LORD to bless you,

Woman,

Because now,

I can call you a mother.

My Mother".

I NEVER KNEW HIM

I never knew him.

But I heard of him,

On that last,

One day of 1994.

An accident occurred,

You see,

At Williams Delight.

A vehicle was passing heading East,

At an intersection,

While a vehicle also heading Eastward,

And in front,

Was making a right turn.

When an officer arrived,

He found a young man,

10 years old,

To be exact,

With what he (the Officer) described as,

"With a weak pulse".

"Control", the officer stated.

"Send the Ambulance A.S.A.P."

Was what was heard from the Officer.

Over the airwaves;

"What is the 20 (location) of the Ambulance"?

Hours later,

At the Police Sub-station,

I asked about him,

The 10 year old,

Who, I'd never seen or heard of,

Until that last day, of December 31, 1994.

I asked the Officer, "How is the boy?"

"He died, the Officer exclaimed.

"He had no visible injuries,

But he was bleeding internally,

He just rolled his eyes back,

And he died"!

On that last day of 1994,

Alone I sat,

Shedding tears,

For a young man

I never knew.

A young man that should have lived

To see a New Year, January 1, 1995.

May he rest in Peace in GOD's realm.

(An un-known Memory).

I AM A FINE GIRL (SONG)

I am a fine girl

Ready to dance tango (off boy)

It is my future

Heavy, on the sound now.

I have no limits

That-sky,

Cannot-hold-me

Like shining stardust

lighting, in the dark night.

I am a fine girl

Living to have fun now

Singing my, lungs off

Sexy, with a tango.

Come on and pop now

Mix the music in me

My heart is aching,

Aching, to the nice beat.

Come on and dance boy

Let me feel your heart beat

Let us mix the tango

With a pop. And to my heart beat.

Spoken: Let us dance
Now to the beat
Let us mix the tango with a pop
And hear my heart and soul beat.

Come on and dance boy
Let me feel your hard heat.
Let us mix the tango
With a pop. And to my heart beat.

Let us make a new sound
That will make all minds roll
Forget all the old songs
Come and try my new beat
Come and dance with the beat
To the beat now, off pop tango.

Spoken: I am a fine girl,
come and dance with me.

Hand in Plate, The Last Super

WHEN I SAY

When I say,

I love you,

When I think,

Of your every breathe,

All my senses,

Feel all the warmth,

And my angels,

Come down to you.

When I say,

I need you,

When I feel,

Your heart's content,

Then I know,

Your love is great,

And your love,

is Pure to give.

When I pray,

I send my angels,

To protect,

Your every dream,

And I know,

That every dream,

Is protecting

Your love

Your soul.

When I say,

I love you,

All my trust,

I put in you,

And I know,

That every day,

Your love grows,

In our souls.

Girl,

When I think of you,

My heart and soul

I gave you.

My love for you

Grows like the universe

And my heart beats

Just for you.

When I say,

I love you,

I mean it,

Forever.

ALWAYS CRYING

I've been told,

Numerous times,

Throughout my life,

That I am always crying.

Well,

I have no apologies,

For I cry,

To feel content,

To help release the sorrows,

Of my heart,

Of the pain,

Down deep within,

And to cleanse,

My soul,

Spirit and mind.

Crying assures my being,

That I will forever,

Overcome my misfortunes,

My nightmares,

Bad times,

And somehow

Someday be happy,

And to enjoy the rest of my life,

In total harmony,

Being humble,

With dignity.

Crying kills,

The dying pain,

That lived within,

And it heals,

And assists me,

In arriving in realms,

Of reality,

That those,

Who do not cry,

Can never achieve,

Arrive to,

Or humble in.

For it is a true fact,

That the LORD,

"JESUS CHRIST"

Humbly cried for us,

To cleanse our sins,

With His blood,

And His last dying breathe,

Directly from the cross.

A CAT NAMED LOVE

(A short untrue story)

Sometime ago, my wife brought home a cat. Since the cat was very playful and affectionate, I eventually called her "Love".

One day, Love climbed up a Mango tree. After attempting to rescue, Love, and unable to get her down for half a day, concerned about her safety, I immediately called the Virgin Islands Fire Department.

About half hour after I called, two Crucian Firemen arrived at my yard. I then proceeded to explain to both, that Love was up in the Mango tree. Both Firemen, wearing big fire hats, without looking up the tree, stared at each other, and then they both looked at me.

Surprised, and amazed one of them proceeded to state, "Sir, we all know that Love is up there, and when he is ready, "GOD", will come down by himself one day. So do us a favor, please don't call us for Love any more".

The Firemen left, and immediately after, Love came down from the tree. Three weeks later, I received via the airmail a fine of $500.00 from the Fire Department, for coming to Love's rescue and answering the call.

A couple of days later, I was at a supermarket, with Love, in my arms. I was petting Love, while a lady was passing by.

Without thinking, I proceeded to tell Love, "I Love you pussy" and before I could say, "Cat" the young lady, proceeded to slap me. She insulted me and immediately called the Virgin Islands Police Department. A V. I. Police Officer arrived at the scene. The lady then proceeded to file a complaint of sexual harassment against me. The Officer then arrested me under the local sexual harassment code.

Yesterday, after I posted $1,000.00 bail, I went to the house. I got ready to go to work, and I decided to carry Love to work with me.

I arrived late to work and was petting Love in the presence of some co-workers. I put Love on the floor, and Love started to purr and brush herself against my legs. Feeling compassionate for my little cat, I proceeded to tell Love, "I love you".

A female co-worker, thinking I was referring to her, slapped me several times, and she immediately called 911.

To my surprise, the same police officer that took the first harassment complaint against me, arrived to my work place. My co-worker filed another harassment complaint against me. I immediately got arrested for a second time in less than three weeks. The officer spoke to the companies' manager, and I got fired immediate-ly and eventually sue for sexual harassment.

After sleeping in jail for a couple of days, I was carried before a judge by the same officer. The judge, who advised me of my rights, decided to lock me up for several weeks, because I was unable to post the $5,000.00 bail. A month later, my case was scheduled for trail.

On the day of the trail, after waiting for eight hours, sleepy, hungry, thirsty and broke, the Clerk of the Court finally called my case, "Government of the Virgin Islands v me, myself and I."

The prosecutor laid out his case and proceeded to call the two complainants and the police officer as witnesses.

I immediately objected by stating; "objection, your honor". The judge then asked for me to place my reason for the objection on the record, to which I proceeded to reply, your Honor, "I just wanted to see if objections really work". The judge warned me he would send me to jail and then proceeded to permit the prosecutor to rest his case.

The prosecutor rested and it was finally my turn to present my defense. Unaware that I should have hired a thief (I mean, an attorney), I proceeded to my opening statements. "I stated, your Honor," I explained, "this matter has to do with Love".

"Even though, both cases are separate from each other, both are connected by Love".

The judge immediately and rudely interrupted. "Sir" he stated. "These are very serious charges against You. I will not tolerate this kind of behavior in my court. Tell you what, to make a long story short, you are guilty as charged and I sentence you to one year in jail, on each charge, which I'm pretty sure you wouldn't love."

After 2 years I jail, and loosing thousands of dollars, my job and reputation, I got out of jail. I arrived to what was my house.

When I arrived, I discovered that my wife was now my ex-wife as soon as I was permitted to enter the living room.

I observed Love on what was my favorite couch. I immediately and without thinking, kicked Love out of my ex-couch and my ex-house.

My ex-wife, called 911. To my surprise, the same police officer, that had arrested me twice two years before, arrived at my ex-house.

I am now a-waiting to be sentenced to five years in jail, before the very judge, without the possibility of bail, and in solitary confinement, on the charge of cruelty to animals, all because of "Love".

(THE MORALE OF THIS STORY)

The morale of this story is: "That if you LOVE or hate pussy (cats), you better don't abuse them. And if you do abuse them, **immediately**, and quickly move to a country, where there exist no extradition treaties with the United States of America, (Go to Castro's Cuba) because you might just end up meeting, the same cop (police officer) the same judge, and the same pussycat, all of the time.

I rest my case. "LOL".

WHY EVERYTHING?

Babies are born each day,

And they grow up to be young adults.

That's when they have a question,

That no one has answered yet!

They think and look for answers,

They search and try with the latest news.

They wonder for years,

But may never come near,

To that Holy,

But, powerful answer.

Because He is OMNIPOTENT,

Only GOD could gave the answers.

He has written them in the BIBLE,

With, which answers', He has filled.

"Why everything?"

Has been the Question,

Which some People,

Might answer in part.

Centuries will pass,

Centuries will go,

But that sacred,

And powerful answer,

Will be answered,

When the end has come near.

Lots of parts form that question.

One involves just Adam and Eve.

The other questions,

May never be answered,

Till the day of our death.

I now come to the conclusion,

Which may never be correct.

But the question,

Just leads to other unanswered questions,

Which are partially correct?

THE LAST DEPARTURE

"Lord,

While being in your presence,

Today I ask for your blessings,

Because my life is almost over,

And for that reason,

This will be,

My last Prayer."

"It is hard to say good bye,

Because in life you appreciate,

And you love,

And departures are very sad,

From the loved ones,

Who've given their hearts,

And the persons

That one wants and one loves

And one admires with devotion".

"The last prayer,

That there will be,

Between you,

My GOD and I,

Will be very sad and hurtful,

But happily I ask,

That you bless and protect,

All of my loving People,

And at the same time,

And with my last breathe,

I ask, YOU,

My loving GOD,

That YOU take me

In YOUR GRACEFUL ARMS,

In this,

My Last Departure".

"Isabel, I know you are in GODS' grace".

This poem was written as a petition from the now deceased Mrs. Isabel Sanabria, on February 2, 1990. Mrs. Sanabria on that date asked me to write her a poem, she stated, "Eddie, I want you to write me a poem of a departure, so that you could read it to me, after I die." I wrote the poem in Spanish and gave her a copy.

The comment was made in Spanish, at her house and front of her daughter "Dali".

Ten years after, Mrs. Sanabria did ask me for a copy of the poem, again in her house in front of her daughter Dali, who was visiting her mother.

I did give a copy to Mrs. Sanabria, and shortly thereafter she died of pulmonary disease. To my surprise, I was asked to read the poem by her loved ones, which I did with all the sadness of my heart and in tears.

Dedicate to Mrs. Isabel Sanabria, my good friend. May you rest in Peace and in GOD's grace.

PEACE BEFORE

How cannot?

The powerful,

Make such an easy choice.

When Humanity cries silently,

Just begging for another chance,

Another year,

Another day.

Why not choose life?

Instead of death,

And beauty,

Before the ugly direction,

That is being forced,

And given onto mankind?

Why not?

I ask!

The powerful of the World,

Choose,

Peace before,

Total world destruction

And annihilation?

DON'T GIVE UP

Don't give up

When things are hard

Don't give up

When your friends are far.

Chorus:

Don't give up,

Don't give up,

Be strong and love

Don't   give up.

Sometimes in life

Life treats you wrong

Its when you fall

When things are hard.

But just have faith

And don't you cry

Quickly look up

And pray to GOD (JAH)

Wo, wo, wo....

Chorus:

Don't give up,

Don't give up,

Be strong and love

Don't give up.

Just look for strength

And look up to JAH

When friends are far

Yeah, very far.

He cures your mind

So you can walk

And gives you love

Right from his heart.

Yeeeeeeeeahhhhhhhh

He shall come

And pick his people

Now do you belong

Will you follow Jahs' heart

Yeaahhhhhhhhh

Will you follow , Jah

"IT' BE, THE LAST TIME"

If I knew

"It' be the last time"

I would hold

You in my arms

I would kiss you

One more time

And never let go.

If I knew

"It' be the last time,"

I would look into your eyes

And I would beg my every breathe

To love you

Forever.

I would fall

Right to my knees

And ask you

To forgive me

And love me

Once again.

I would pray ... to GOD

For the greatest love of all

And a miracle

That if one day, you would leave
You would return, to me, once again.

I would ask a shining star
To guide you with its light
And return you to my arms
And my kisses, one more time.

I would appreciate
Every breathe that you take
Forever more
And fall asleep
So silently
In your arms
While feeling your heart beat
And looking into your eyes.

I would hold you in my arms
I would kiss you
One more time
And never let go
If I knew
"It' be the last time"

Jesus Christ at the Garden of Gethsemane

WALK BESIDES ME

Come to me,

Walk besides me,

Learn to love,

Me every breathe.

Touch my body,

With your hands,

Make me yours,

One day, one year.

Let us grow,

In our quest,

To find real love,

And happiness.

Lets embrace,

Our happy thoughts,

And lets caress,

Both of our souls.

Let us kiss,

Forever and,

Both walk besides,

In complete love.

I ACCEPT YOU

I accept you,

As my love,

To walk besides you,

For ever more.

I want to hold you,

One day, one year,

And for a life time,

Be there for you.

In good and bad times,

For evermore,

And in eternity,

Be only yours.

I know, I'll cherish,

Your every breathe,

And that you will give me,

Your love to keep.

Come and walk besides me,

And hold my hand,

Be mine forever,

My eternity.

Awake besides me,

With all your love,

And hold me in your arms,

Until death,

Do us part.

Come walk with me,

Besides,

In all eternity,

Let us cherish,

Every second and minute,

Of our love.

Let us hold hands,

And kiss forever,

And never let go.

Never let us part,

And before GOD,

Let us love,

Each other,

In all of our eternity.

Come and walk,

Besides me,

And hold my hand,

Be mine forever,

My eternity.

Awake besides me

With all your love

And hold me

In your arms

Until

Death

Do us part.

I'll always love you,

Girl,

For you are my breathe,

My soul,

My heart,

My all.

FIRST DADDIES GIRL
(SONG DEDICATED TO MY DAUGTHER)

Oh, oh, my little girl,

How much I miss you,

You are first daddy's girl,

And then a sailor.

When you walk away from me,

My heart just breaks in two,

I pray to GOD to bless you,

I ask the Lord to keep you.

My angels I send to guard you,

Every time you need of me,

They guard you while you sleep

They guard you, when you dram.

Oh, Oh, my little girl, how have you grown?

You are a sailor, but first daddy's girl.

You will see the world,

Of wars and battles,

You will travel all the high seas,

In mighty ships of battles.

Oh, how much I miss you;

You my only girl.

I will always ask my GOD above,

To bless your beautiful soul,

And I will send my angels',

To watch you every way you go.

Oh, Oh, my little girl, how have you grown?

Your beauty speaks of you; your heart is just like gold.

I've seen your every walk

And I've seen you fall,

My tears will always roll,

When you are not near.

I'll send my angels', to guard you from danger,

I ask my GOD to bless you, and Jesus to guide you.

Oh, oh, my little girl, I can't be without you

My heart belongs to you, everywhere you go.

Oh, Oh, my little girl

How much I love you,

GOD will protect your soul and my angels,

Will watch over you.

YOUR KNIGHT IN
SHINING ARMOR

I want to carry,

The sword of dignity,

To protect you,

Girl from harm,

I want to forge,

The blades that will cut,

Deep within the flesh of knight,

In order to let,

The brilliance of light and beauty,

Safeguard your way,

All of the time.

Please,

Bare with me,

Your knight in shining armor,

Please,

Bare with me,

For I love You,

with all my heart.

I have proven,

So many times,

In the battles,

Of so many other knights',

That love triumphs forever,

And in so many different ways,

Only one man can win,

So I'll try my best,

To be the victor,

As many times,

As you want me,

be your love.

I will win each battle,

I will win each knight,

As long as you want me,

Be your love.

Woman,

This Ex-calibre,

Your knight in shining armor,

Will carry,

To protect you,

With its sharpness,

All the rest,

Of your life.

Your Knight in shining armor.

WE SAY GOODBYE

It's been years,

That you left,

That you're life,

Mind and body,

Don't belong.

It's been years,

That I know,

That your heart,

Does not belong,

To me.

You are there,

In front of me,

But the Love,

Of our past,

Has come to end.

Now we part,

To, our separate ways,

With a good bye,

I pray and wish you,

Girl the best.

Now, I say good bye.

It's been years,

That I left,

That my life,

Mind and body,

Don't belong.

It's been years,

That you know,

That my heart,

Does not belong,

To you.

I am here,

In front of you,

But the love,

Of our past,

Has come to end.

Now we part,

To our separate ways,

With a good bye,

You pray and wish me,

The best.

Now, we say good bye.

"THE WHISPER"

The Whisper of the wind,

Is like the whisper of love.

For many times,

It is heard and felt,

And many other times,

It is accepted

In ones' heart.

But, in my life,

I've found out,

That there are whispers,

That just flow freely

Like the wind

And its breeze

That disappears

And goes away,

Forever and ever,

In our lives.

YOU'VE BEEN MY FRIEND

You've given me,
The star's above.

You've help me soar,
Above the sky.

You've held my hand,
So, I wouldn't fall.

You've stepped behind,
The open doors.

You've been my friend,
When all has failed.

You've held me up,
So, I could walk.

You've been my strength,
My thirst,

My luck,

You've never left,

My side,

My love.

I've pray to GOD,

To keep your soul.

To keep you bless,

With all your love.

You are the sea,

Of harmony.

You are the skies,

Of melodies.

You are my hope,

My sight,

My consciousness,

And all the dreams,

That, have come true.

You are the one,

Who's guide I've had.

The only one,

I'll follow,

Near to my soul,

Near to my....heart.

IN SILENCE

When I find myself in silence,

I find happiness,

Within my thoughts and my life,

For I think of your smile,

Your beautiful eyes,

Which I will keep,

Within my heart.

For in silence,

I withhold,

The true feelings,

Of my heart,

And the desires,

Of my mind.

My soul,

Demands your attention,

Your eyes,

Demand the truth,

Your lips,

Within my dreams,

Demand my kisses,

But every time,

You are before me,

I am awake,

And I lie to my senses.

I make believe,

In all my dreams,

That your lips,

Have a place,

Down and deep inside,

Down very deep and within my heart.

Within my heart,

For in my dreams,

You live therein,

Just awaiting

For me,

My desires,

Love,

And my kisses.

Jesus Christ on the Cross

THE LAST DYING TEAR

It was the last minute of a dying day of any year, when reddish humongous clouds of fiery fire and black smoke appeared in the horizon while the gaseous burning fumes and neutrinos furious blasts of high radioactive energy hid the shining sun, blue sky and clouds.

After a thunderous intolerant roar and unbearable noise, like that of a freight train multiplied by millions of times, it made time stand still. Its' effects appeared to freeze in total darkness and solitude the space around.

Silence stood still, until night was no more, betrayed by the dawn of yet another day in the course of the change of the rotating earth on its now opposite axis.

Seconds and minutes continued to tick, and even though it was now the morning of another day, the sun being born again, fought to find its usual destiny of bringing sun light to humanity, animals, plants and every living creature of land and the oceans. Everything that was alive just one day before.

The now unseen sky and sun were out of sight and hidden by monstrous black clouds of darkness that blinded every sight of every living creature that otherwise would be alive.

The darkness of the clouds dominated everything, and breathing ceased while negative entities filled the atmosphere with a heat storm of over 1,200 degrees, but fully in what should have been a normal, midsummer day of 89 degrees.

The cries of a weak and hungry baby, was heard defying the ever growing silence of death, in the shadows of darkness, while his mother laid curled in a fetus position, with her now death gripe, holding onto the gift of life, her baby, while the fruit of her precious womb, laid besides still breathing, labored and attempting to avoid succumbing to his unforgiving destiny, like all death.

The baby felt not the dying quivers and last breathe of his mother, the day before, for at his 30 days of life, he somehow could not sense the inevitable towards him, and every living thing on the face of the earth. The death of everything at almost the same time of space.

The baby laid protected by his mothers' lifeless body, for her fetus position was what for several hours denied him instant death, for he now laid entrapped besides the motionless chest of the woman who loved him, and did protect him like she swore she would in life, while in her womb.

The baby, who's name no longer mattered, had somehow witnessed the worst destructive act of mans' ignorance, via man's own hand, total annihilation! The end of mankind, yet he knew not.

He had survived the greatest tribulation, not to continue to live, not to grow, nor talk to generations, not to come about to continue living that last day, that last hour, minute and second of his life, but to demand justified hope against the biggest destructive force that the world via mankind, dared inflict and unfold on itself. The greatest harm, vengeance and retaliation on Mother Earth.

Now being the only surviving witness of humanities destructive disappearance, crying, grasping for clean un-existing air, suffering and in pain and burnt beyond recognition, the 30 day old baby, blind, laid unable to move, still in his mother's over protective death trap and gripe.

Gasping, un-freed, he dared not inhale to deep, for he somehow perceived that the air, fill with unknown gasses would eventually kill him. For his death was inevitable and soon to be forth coming in the last nurturing embraceable hold, that of his over protective, loving and once caring mother. Her once caring arms no longer offered protection, but now his quick demise.

The baby could no longer cry. In his silence, because of the burnt injuries to his charred skin inflicted on him by those in authority the day before. Hunger made him weaker by the second and thirstier by the minute and unable to get the attention from no one, least his mother, and hurting like never before in his 30 days of living, he now laid still in his mother's embrace, for her over protective hands would in future seconds, un- fortunately become his tomb.

The silence of death was close to visit, and at last, at noon of that last day, of any giving year, it arrived for an innocent child of GOD, that never did anything hateful against anyone in the world, but somehow, he had also paid with his fragile body and last breathe.

That noon, when he finally dared to bravely take his last breathe of precious life and succumbed to his torturous demeaning, dying faith. A faith that mankind swore never to recognize nor take responsibility for.

For in the immense darkness, stillness, and stench of decaying bodies, nobody lived, to report it. Nobody!

The baby's death was selfishly inflicted via the capricious and willful arbitrary power, of brutal unconsciousness of some men against mankind in ignominy and disrespect towards humanity and total ignorance, for the fight and struggle for total control of destructive and violent power, in mans' selfish domain to mentally conquer all, eventually and inevitably inviting death, there-by failing to produce a winner and total victor.

For even in death, nothing has a price but the awards are just for the living. That is, if any are left!

The baby took his last innocent, but hateful breathe of life, in hopes to continue living, even for the few minutes or seconds more.

Now, the only thing alive and without hope, for it would also succumb to death and perish, was a tear.

A tear that had escaped, prematurely, from the baby's crying eye, like his premature demise while taking his last dying breathe.

But not even the crying tear had a praying chance for life. For it would eventually succumb to and with the dust of the fallout of the final un-intelligent conscious act of brutality towards mankind, it would arrive to a still, failing to move and eventually drying up on the babies' burnt cheek and silenced body.

For it was mankind's last doing, Armageddon and the babies, "last dying tear."

(THE MORALE OF THIS STORY)

Man, in his search for total control and power of anything, stops at nothing. He (she), (they) become manipulators, dictators, in the evilest form, and wicked in their ways to feed the compulsive nature of their inevitable hunger and thirst. For that reason, what they believe is the ultimate high in their lives of power, becomes hatred and dislike against all, in order to achieve his, (her), (their), ultimate performance.

Nothing matters in that quest and he, (she), (they), dare not be obstructed or feel threatened to be obstructed by anyone, anywhere when he, (she), (they), is in search to wield the rein of power.

For ignorance, is betrayal to all, becomes his, (her), (their), ally, un-equivocal and faithful friend, demeanor and wealth of un-intellectual greed surpasses the unimaginable, becoming his, (her), (their), ultimate goal.

It matters not, how destructive he (she), (they), becomes and who or how they hurt other People. It matters not, at that moment, the final outcome.

"THE END, WILL IT BEGIN?"

Silence grew,

When the end,

Grew near.

For hours,

Seemed like seconds,

When the death of the world,

As we know it,

Grew near.

The battle of Armageddon,

Has been predicted,

In this our time,

For 34 have been fought in Gideon,

In the same exact place.

I now ask myself,

Will the next,

Claim a tear?

I wonder all the time,

If those in power,

Ask and seek the truth,

In pair?

Or if their bending of all laws,

Via dishonestly,

Ignominy,

Deceit and manipulation,

Bury the truth,

With their many lies?

Oh, Dear God,

I ask, You as of why?

As of why?

Society and its' masses,

Permits a hand full,

Of wicked and vicious men,

Who are only and the few,

And who hide behind the truth,

With their commitment,

To wars in falsehood,

too hide their many lies?

I ask Thy, My Lord,

If they have ever,

Ask them-selves,

The greatest question of all,

"The end,

Will it begin?

When? 4/8/07@2230

KNOWINGLY PROCEEDS

When a judge,

Or other men in authority,

Knowingly proceed(s),

Against another man,

Without cause,

He not only condemns himself,

And the man,

But also the system of justice,

And in disparity,

Inflicts past wounds of slavery,

Oppression,

Racism,

And tyranny,

Turning the hands of the clock,

Of injustices past,

And barbaric prejudices,

Towards the future.

The system then crumbles,

And shakes in fear and agony,

Like and imprisoned soldier and country at war,

Fighting with its enemies,

Or like an island,

Devastated and touched by a powerful earthquake,

Where-in the power,

Of the trembling ground,

Becomes arrogant and defiant,

Towards the balance of Mother Nature,

Breaking and crumbling with its tremors,

Lady Liberty and The Magna Carta of the land,

Its laws and it's correct,

Applicability's.

Lady Justice is inflicted,

With the harsh lies,

And the living venom of,

A disease called hatred,

With blatant racist,

Implications,

Towards the man and mankind,

This without proper justification,

Or a cause,

And or a logical,

Explanation.

The venom,

Swells her heart,

With unclean blood,

And her breathe becomes shallow,

And eventually stops,

Like a dying hunger,

And thirst of a dying tear.

When her now darkened heart stops,

Her thoughts die,

For the corrupt dare to contradict,

The intellect of a humble and crying soul,

And in ignorance and betrayal,

Kills Lady Justices' wisdom,

And the very principal,

And the very honor,

Of that judge,

Who once,

Swore,

To protect.

The Honor of Lady Justice,

The one that with the truth,

Of wisdom and understanding,

Overlooks the saving of,

Mankind from total annihilation

And destruction,

Deny not only the man,

Of justice,

But also them-selves,

And their own future generations,

And the true meaning of the letter,

Of the law.

The slaying of the lady

With her own,

Double edged sword,

That which equals,

The intellectual death,

Of their own ignorant mind,

And Future generations.

For the death,

Via deplorable nonsense,

And ignorance,

Of those who once,

Swore to protect,

Via the blinded, "Lady Justice",

Bury in the crumbling laws of humanity,

With lies via defiance,

And in black robes strike,

With destructive force,

 At those that knowingly fight,

The fools of complete circumstance and ignorance!

THE SCALE OF JUSTICE

The balance,

via the scale of justice,

Will tip and topple to one side.

It will be full of blood on one side,

And of the secret indulgence of many,

On the other.

Those who intellectually proceed contrary,

And hidden behind,

Darken and cold places,

Against her mighty will,

And powerful sword.

The Supreme will collapse,

For the foundation

Of the lower courts of justice,

Has crack's, crevasses'

And crumbling concrete of dishonestly,

And disregard for those,

That begs for just one day,

And their desire to be heard,

Before a court.

Slavery will be painful,

Slow and agonizing for the poor masses,

While the high sight of the eyes,

Of the wicked,

Arrives to protect others,

In high places.

The sight of all opposed,

Will search and look at the dirt,

Under their feet,

For the sight arrives completely,

At the end of the Mayan calendar.

The top of the halls of Justice,

Will topple,

Crumble and fall,

And an unbalanced,

Government of uncertainty,

Will oppress like,

Never seen and lived before.

The order will be unstoppable,

And in a fierce attacking rage,

Will put many at hunger,

Pain, suffering, disgrace and death,

Then many will ask the question,

"Why LORD, did I stand in line so silently,

Avoiding the rocking of the boat,

In a sea of uncertainty and in tranquility,

For so long to avoid the coming pain,

The one I must now defend against?"

The vicious will devour from within,

Rome and the Halls of the Vatican,

Where-in darkness exist will hunt towards,

Those whose hearts are pure and clean.

People of the world,

Double in hunger,

In numbers and masses,

Ready to see the coming of Armageddon,

On the 12th year

Of the new millennium,

Then Christianity will suffer,

And there will be many,

Hypocrites for convenience,

Willing to staying on the right,

For their hypocrisy will only equal,

Not only betrayal,

But pain, suffering and humiliation,

To their brothers and sisters,

Mothers' and fathers

Friends and lovers,

Sons and daughters,

For the side to punish is the left,

To protect their dark

And un-scrupulous soul(s).

Those who dare stand,

Shall either die fighting,

Or hidden from

The venom of their oppressors.

Christians will suffer profusely,

And start dying a slow,

But tyrannical death,

For it will befall,

Amongst its own members.

The status quo seeks,

To stand tall and mighty,

For the vile and powerful,

Evil, cold calculated hearts,

Will feel no sorrows.

The end of the good willed men,

Will come to cease,

For they stand unfortunate,

In the way of progress,

And of the minority,

Of the new culture,

Of vicious and greedy hearts,

Never seen before.

Fewer men will be born,

And the sequence of life,

Will grow towards maturity for some,

While life will be conceived,

In hidden labs of a new,

And controlled race.

For science will control,

The evolution of man,

To and almost total destruction,

For the thought process of the Nazi's,

Lives in hidden minds of society today,

And racism lives on breathing uncontrollably,

And will never die against many.

Tears will befall,

And blood will be shed,

In the name of progress,

But the land will feel the hurt,

And sorrow of the people,

And become un-fertile.

The way of,

And the beast,

Will indeed challenge GOD,

And Arch Angel Michael.

Society as we know it,

Will cry and be no more. 7/14/08@1920

(THE MORALE OF THIS POEM)

"Be very careful who you stand besides, and what side you choose to stand on. For you might unknowingly be standing in the line of the silent, awaiting for the chip to be put in place, there-by betraying every one you love, to include but not limit, first the love of GOD.

It is good, that you as a Christian attend services, whatever belief you belong to. I do warning that many who believe in GOD, will be the first ones to cross the line, to serve not GOD but mammon, for hunger and thirst will force them to choose unwisely.

It will be your choice, and only your choice, to pick a side. Persecution(s) will be harsh against those to the left, those with clean hearts, minds and souls. Those that have given their souls to only GOD.

I am aware that some things within this my first book, are controversial in nature. I only ask you, to pick the side of the living GOD, Almighty, no matter what the consequence(s). GOD bless"

The death of the Christ

THE PENDULUM OF INJUSITCE

The pendulum of injustice,

Does not recognize nor perceive,

A truthful and honest time,

In which Civil Rights violations,

Will cease or decrease.

For a majority,

Ride and stand on the negative,

Side of the pendulum,

Via convenience,

Preventing the end of injustices,

Of slavery.

Dominance and disrespect,

Slowly kill and stop

The movement and power

Of Civil Rights,

While a small minority,

Fight against the pendulum,

Demanding justice,

And via its' swinging force,

Demanding a created friction,

Against the oppressors,

Then, a new majority is indeed born.

The minority will stand

in defense of the cause,

for justice,

carrying a crushing,

painful and very heavy,

slowly and dying burden.

The minority

Must be strong,

To stand against the giant,

The majority,

For it matters not,

The minorities' numbers,

What really matters,

Is a stand for the truth.

A stand that will indeed,

Influence with integrity,

The correct standing of society's ills

In a true new and proper direction.

The minority,

Must in an intellectual way,

Convince the Majority

That the destructive path,

And negative wealth of ignorance, arrogance,

Will eventually crumble,

and disintegrate to nothing,

It will hurt all,

And will not pick individual sides,

For there must always be a minority.

The Majority in ignominy,

Does not realize,

That it dooms itself,

Individually, separated,

And that the pendulum favors all,

And in a respectable sense,

For the pendulum swings,

Indiscriminately for all un-blindly,

But it is the minds of the majority,

That uses ignorance, blindly,

To intimidate and control everything,

To include that,

What should positively favor all.

All that opposes (the minority),

Must indeed be destroyed and extinguished,

No matter the consequences. 11/09/06@1058

A BIRTHDAY CONVERSATION

"Hey Eddie, the other day, someone told me that it was your birthday. That you had just turned 60, so unable to believe what that person told me, I had to somehow approach you, because I didn't believe him".

"So Eddie, even though you look 30, he told me that you are 60, should I believe him? Please tell me that you are not 60".

Eddie immediately replied. "No Eddie, that was just a worthless rumor, how could I be 60, if I only turned 30?

He then continued; "You should not believe everything that you hear, the person who told you that I was 60, is only 2 years younger than me". "You see Eddie" he continued, "because he always knew that I was older, he just did a simple, mathematical and multiplication equation."

"He took the 2 years difference between him and myself, and he multiplied my 30 years of life, by 2 which is the difference between our ages." "So 30 multiplied by 2 equal 60. That is why he rumored that I was 60 or twice his age. Comprend?"

"Well Eddie, it's kind of complicated, but I thank you for explaining that you are only 30 and not 60." See you later." And Eddie replied, "Good bye" and he merrily walked away, leaving me with this dumb old and stupid story and its' morale, summed up below.

THE MORALE OF THIS STORY

"If you are standing around 2 Puerto Rican individuals, who are also Crucians that have nothing to do, in the middle of no-where, at 2 in the morning and none of the 2 are dancing Salsa or drinking Crucian Rum by a beautiful beach, with a girlfriend. I give you this advice." "Please, but please, mind your own business, to avoid the big confusion of reading the Morale of this STORY. Don't listen in to the crazy conversation of 2 cousins whose both names are "Eddie" ", and this there true story."

"I'm pretty sure Confucius would have been confused also."

WHEN DARKNESS SETTLES

When darkness settles,

In the heart, soul and mind of a man,

He sees not,

The light before him,

For he becomes blinded

In the very darkness and abyss,

That he, himself has created.

For he fails to see

With the true eyes of the mind,

There-by find the true and correct meaning,

And values of the written word,

Be it verbal,

Or written or understood,

And the true deeds of his

Tarnished heart and lost soul.

Un-cleanly-ness lives within,

For he seeks in darkness to hide,

For the reflection of

his eyes remain hidden

For there exist no light

To make his eyes shine

For shame is his love of life

His heart and soul

Becomes and there-by remains

Perpetrated and black as charcoal.

That is the way of a man,

With a dark and unreflective mind,

And a rotten corrupt, venomous and vicious soul.

To remain,

Where no light shines or exist,

For his secret

Lives where nothing can be seen,

In the universal corners of darkness

And of nothing,

And in his ill egotistic reflection(s)

Of his self image,

And his image alone.

That of ignorance and with malice

Aforethought of his own

Dark and buried

Un-intellectual consciousness

Ignoramescenti wearing a black robe

Of dishonesty with an impeachable

Distorted and confused mind.

THE STRANGE MAN

Once in my life, there came to exist, a strange man. When I was young, he would hold me in his arms, and he loved me. He was chosen to show me about life. The one who'd talk to me about friendships, and love. Many years passed by, and my hopes of learning about life and many other things, faded, because the man, that strange man, who for many years walked besides me and promised to show me many things, by educating me, left, I understood then, without meaning.

Allegedly, the strange man had a problem once. I had come to admire him as I grew, and I knew he sought to teach me many things. How to play and to walk in his protective shadow, how to take the correct road and direction in life, how to love every second of every breathe that I took, and how to love nature and people, without judgments. He even showed me how to work, so that I would become a productive man of good.

He did promise to be patient at my side, and to correct my mistake. He'd help me up, when I fell down, he'd calm my soul when I was sad, and made he made me laugh in joy with positive charms.

He showed me how, to always say the truth, no matter how much the situation I thought merited a lie, and how to respect thy neighbors' property, and all those important things, that a young person should learn about respecting authority, all this he did, before I arrived at maturity.

One day, I noticed how the strange man would treat me differently than other children that he had. I then began to feel the lack of love, and daily necessities after he left. At special moments, when I mostly needed him, on my birthdays, my graduations, Christmas, I no longer saw him and thus I started to miss him.

That Man that I loved with all my heart, and I was starting to know as I grew, was now a complete stranger. No don't misunderstand me. I was his bloodline and exact image. I was his own reflection.

Now, at his point in my life, I felt, that in his thoughts, I did not exist. For he stopped being around me, and loyally loving me, like he did in the past, what I thought then that he saw in me, was the unnecessary spending of his resources, his strength, and his love, wisdom and money on me.

One day, the strange man found himself on his death bed. Now sad, alone and desperate and depressed, he sent for me. It had been many years that I'd seen and or heard of him, for he failed to even share precious moments and quality times around me. He ignored me and that I failed to understand. Why I asked? Why he so dishonestly disappeared. And that I failed to understand.

That day, that he found himself in his death bed, he remembered me, and that afternoon, my mother told me that the stranger, had prayed to the "Lord Jesus", asking for forgiveness for he knew now, that it was improper for him to have disappeared, from my life, the way he did. She then begged me to go to his side, where she knew he would never leave alive. His death bed.

I then looked at the reflection of myself in a mirror and I saw his image, where my image should have been. I then decide not to go before him, to his death bed.

Now egotistic and an adult, guided by what I had wrongfully learned, I decided to give him a lesson of love.

But with lots of respect, I sent a message, which was very profound, strongly worded, to the strange man, where-in I stated: "Sir, I am very sorry, I cannot go to your side in this your time of need, besides your death bed, but I learned that from you many years ago, when you were not there by my side when I needed you most. When I cried uncontrollable-ly for I missed you so. That one day I became a stranger to you when you hurt my soul. That one day I shall never forget, for you unequivocally stopped sharing your love and life with me."

"Now, I state to you, in these last minutes and seconds of your life, I have to unfortunately inform you and pay you with the same coin you once paid me. "Your own coin".

"Because you abandoned me, while I was a young growing boy, without your company, for so many years, and remembering that you failed at all times to assist me, not only monetary but with your strength full and caring love and hands, when I was weak, hungry and when I fell and when I cried for, I wanted to see you".

"Today I let you know, that I died in life, while I grew up, just like today, in the next several minutes and seconds of your life, in life you will die".

"Father, strange man. Today I tell you, that I love you, and without a heavy heart towards you and in my soul, I let you know, that I treat you now, the same way that you treated me, in your ignorance, in your past".

When, I knew that he'd read the letter, I walked into his room and told him, "I forgive you dad." I kissed him on his cheeks, I held him for what seemed like a life time. He looked at me then told me, "I love you son, and forgive me". As soon as I said, "I forgive you, dad" then he quietly and peacefully passed away.

It was amazing how I felt then. I cried, not because he died, but because I knew that those few minutes that I held him in my arms, those few seconds, I cherished and loved him, like never before and I knew that I held Him in his death bed, like he had held me minutes after I was born. In his strong, rough, caring, loving hands.

He'd even showed me the hardest lesson that I had learn in a short instance of life and love, from his death bed. The lesson that "we should all forgive, those who in life trespass against us", like the living Christ did.

For to carry the heavy burden of hate, we darken our souls, and our life stinks and swells of anger and then the betrayal and retaliation becomes our only focus and eventual existence though out life.

THE MORALE AND REFLECTION OF THIS STORY

Life is so short, that many times in the blink of and eye, it ceases to exist without warning. To destroy one self walking in the imprints of ignorance and darken shadows and in the wrong direction, via retaliation, only makes us more furious and disheartening for our hearts become black as coal, and our mouths and minds make us look like those that (we believe) did us wrong.

We gain nothing but the illness of the heart, bodies, and darken soul(s), and lost spirit of light to guide us towards un-true love and un-enlightened knowledge.

The intelligent and intellectual man is he who pardons another and clears him (the man) if he has done nothing wrong, and who realizes that in order to proceed towards a possible punishment, for any reason against the accused, there must be stated cause and witnesses who will come forth, without lies to tell the truth.

Many times I asked myself, should I proceed towards my enemy's like they have proceeded against me? Only one statement is true from my heart and soul. That I have cause to proceed against them, yet, I reflect on how foolish I would be, to pay them with the same coin of ignorance.

For it is ignorance of a studied man and unkindly-ness that which makes him a total fool, not before his audience and allies, but before those that he/she transgresses and proceeded against.

There are fools of opportunity, fools of choice, fools of pure ignorance, fools who follow others because they are not leaders for they only learned to follow. Fools who believe they are in full power and control, yet they are only puppets in high places who wear black robes, and being told how to run their high chair(s) of indifference and bounties of disrespect and treachery, treason, in their sinking ship of lies and arrogance.

There are fools of conspiracies. Fools blinded by the power of their sworn positions, and office they hold.

It is however a pity and disgrace, of how many followers, follow as fools, the fools who walk in front of them without direction, walking hand in hand with vile and darken individuals who violate every law of the land and rules. Rules of the very court that they change for their very satisfaction and betrayal to the honor that what they swore to protect.

For it is in their wicked, tarnished minds, that we find weaknesses in their attacks against he who demands justice, and who dares stand alone with a pen as a weapon against the mighty blinded sword of ignominy and shame of Lady Justice. Those fools that sit applying the reversed laws of ignorance and convenience against the very Constitution that they swore to protect are fools of disloyalty, racist towards the human race and court.

To sit in judgment of another, one must be fair and none judgmental, without biasness in a neutral frame of mind. To believe as a judge that he has triumphed because he has hidden with distorted lies, the truth, means nothing to the deprived individual.

Money and power isn't everything for it is a fools' way of losing his soul, and intellect, and breathe of life.

Today, I dedicate this "Morale and reflection" and I wonder, what in hell was I thinking when I was looking up to the many People, Judges, Lieutenant

Governor and Attorney(s) that I once as a fool admired and protected and would have as a Police Officer given my life for, to protect?

Today, I forgive those who without cause have proceeded against me, protecting the fools that make them look like fools. My best friend and companion, the pen(s) that I've used to pen this, my 1st book bares witness.

I thank every fool that has contributed to my success, for without any of you this book and thoughts here-in would not be possible. Here-in I further state: "I shall not be like you, like the reflection of the mirror."

"Thank "God" that I was not foolish enough to give my life to protect any of yours. I forgive you."

WHILE SPEAKING TO YOU

While speaking to you

A paralegal,

Our conversation strayed

From one thought

To many others.

I suddenly asked you,

To help me understand,

Some of my questions

And comments.

How can you deal

With the outdated, distorted,

Contradicting laws of the Land?

I asked.

I then noticed

That you sought silence

Cause my questions

Just keep coming.

Tell me,

Can society be wrong?

In many a number of ways?

What is humanities goal,

in this our world?

Was the U. S. Constitution

Written for some and not for all,

And does it wrongfully start

As "We the People?"

Does Racism Exist?

In some person's mind

And does hatred have a place

In some Peoples' hearts?

I paused for a few moments

And then I continued to comment,

Peace on earth will never be

Cause everyone has battles to fight

And a lot of wars

To win or lose.

There is a lot of crime,

And no respect or justice

While pride and honor

Are words of the past?

And racism and apartheid

Are both words of the day?

While civil rights

Have unbalanced the scale

And lawmakers keep changing the laws

To protect the criminal offenders

While the victims

Continue to live in fear

And the laws of our land

Continue to tie

The long arms of the law.

Our leaders and government

Keep the people oppressed

By starving the children

And adults to death.

The Death and Rise Of the Christ

SLAVERY

The word slavery has almost,

Disappeared from our vocabulary.

It has broken out from its' cocoon

Into what we now know as

Oppression, Discrimination,

Retaliation, Human and Civil Rights violations,

Degradation, disrespect, demotions,

And illegal terminations,

Among other kinds of mistreatments,

Of the modern work place.

Speak not against these evils,

And you shall eventually feel,

Its wicked and vile and venomous bite,

Somewhere within your life,

Via the slandering snake of persecution.

The slave master from the ranks,

Represents and hides those in charge,

In high and darken places,

But he's trapped as the weakest,

Which makes him the strongest?

And demands via the strike of the invisible,

Whip of threatened uncertainty,

To forcefully produce

And make the 5 percent rich.

For to exploit 95 percent of the populous,

Is the biggest game of the day?

With turning eyes avoiding contact,

In hypocrisy of broken laws

and binding contracts.

Caring for who you work for,

Is a big hoax of yester years?

And dishonesty and disrespect

From the powers to be,

Are the norm of the day.

For they file must remain

Committed and loyal to the rank

With begging hearts and silenced

Souls' without talk.

But dare beg for what is rightfully yours

And the wipe of un-certainty

Shall strike you towards poverty

Homelessness and financial disaster,

For silence is demanded

And to challenge they say degrades them

They hide in high places of power

That makes the slave master

swing his whip uncontrollably

To every man and woman

Who here-in read my words,

Gain strength in God

And prepare thy souls

For what is to come

Is it the whip of disaster?

The whip of despair,

The whip of slave masters,

Who's laugh are in high places,

Thinking and planning,

In what is to come,

Without a majority in mind.

Go forth and see the world,

Let no man show you,

The wrong direction,

Come out of the roach hole,

And rat hole that you live in,

And see and educate yourself,

Open your mind,

Body and soul to the consciousness

Of the Lord, Jesus Christ,

And search for,

And find the truth.

Stare clear of those,

That in their best interest,

Somehow are,

Willing to indeed misguide you,

And teach you their vile and wicked ways.

The heart and mind are separate and usually in conflict with each other even though both are relatively connected. The heart desires and does things via impulse, for it knows not its true destiny, without though to any upcoming future consequences. The minds' though process, filters via reality, and many times attempts to stop us from reacting to our hearts' impulses. Un-fortunately our hearts react quicker leaving our minds to clean up the un-necessary mess and disasters, especially when it has to do with love.

TODAY

Today, it started to rain very hard. The clouds returned and then turned grey, the wind then blew, while the sun stayed hid. Your smile came into my mind, I then remembered that first bright lovely day, back in June 11, 1984 that day that you brought joy into my heart, into my soul.

That first year that so quickly went by, that almost noon when you were no longer a child, and that afternoon when as a young lady, now a soldier you laid your head, on my lap, tired and exhausted after your graduation from the Navy when in the back seat of a rental car you curled yourself like that baby.

That baby I once held in my arms, my joy, my love, there now asleep for the last time on daddies lap in years gone by, while the song, Butterfly Kisses played.

That beautiful song that let me know, that daddy's girl was now a woman about to fall in love. Overjoyed like a proud dad I cried. I cried of joy, for you had achieved your new goal, and career.

You are my gift. That gift which would bring my second gifts into my life.

They who in my childhood dreams I never dreamt of meeting they that lived once within your wound.

The morning greeted the day once again, and my thoughts returned to present. I saw a rainbow, clearly in the sky.

Some hours passed, and the rain just slowed down, as the dusk of the morning grew near, the rain, then came to a trickle. It is another beautiful day, as I looked up to the sky, the rain stopped, and unknowing to my eyes, I saw the last rain drop, fall before my eyes.

To order the poster of "The Question" or any of the prints here-in and prices contact Edwin Gautier Vega via E-mail @ e5d5i5e5@yahoo.com